THE VILLAGE AND THE SPIDER THAT GREW AND GREW

THE VILLAGE AND THE SPIDER THAT GREW AND GREW

Jordan Rivers

Illustrated by Arkie Ring

Rivers Ink, LLC.   •   Chicago, Illinois

Rivers Ink, LLC.,
Chicago, Illinois 60661
www.RiversInk.com

ISBN: 978-0-692-29274-7
LCCN: 2014951254

Cover designed and illustrations by Arkie Ring
Text design and composition by John Reinhardt Book Design

Printed in the United States of America

Jeremiah & Joshua

Always remember the bigger the problem the bigger the Blessing

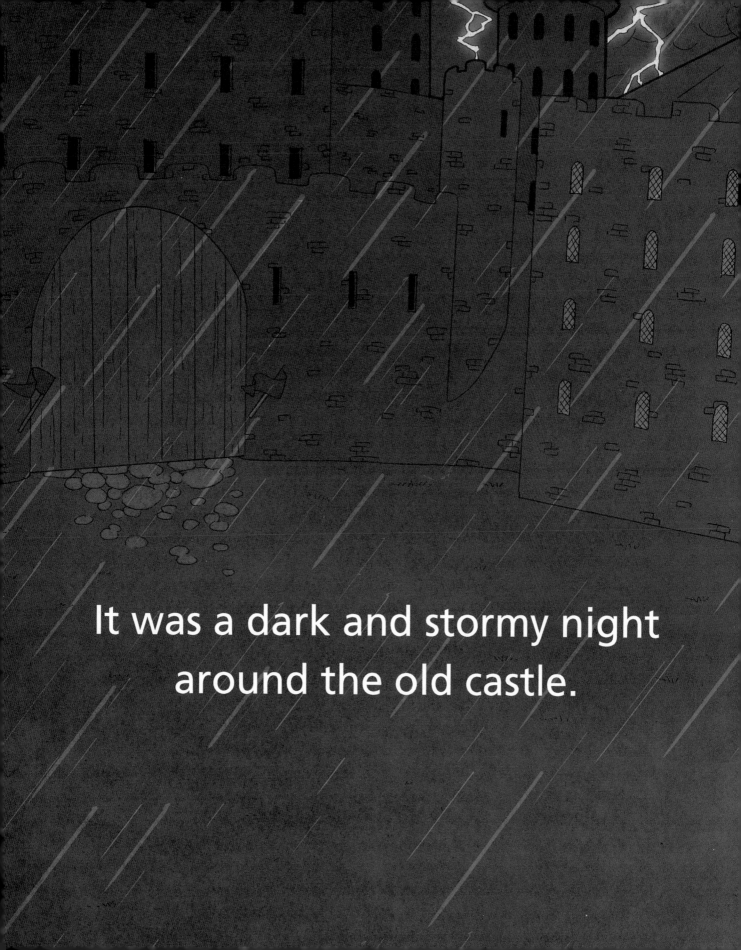

It was a dark and stormy night around the old castle.

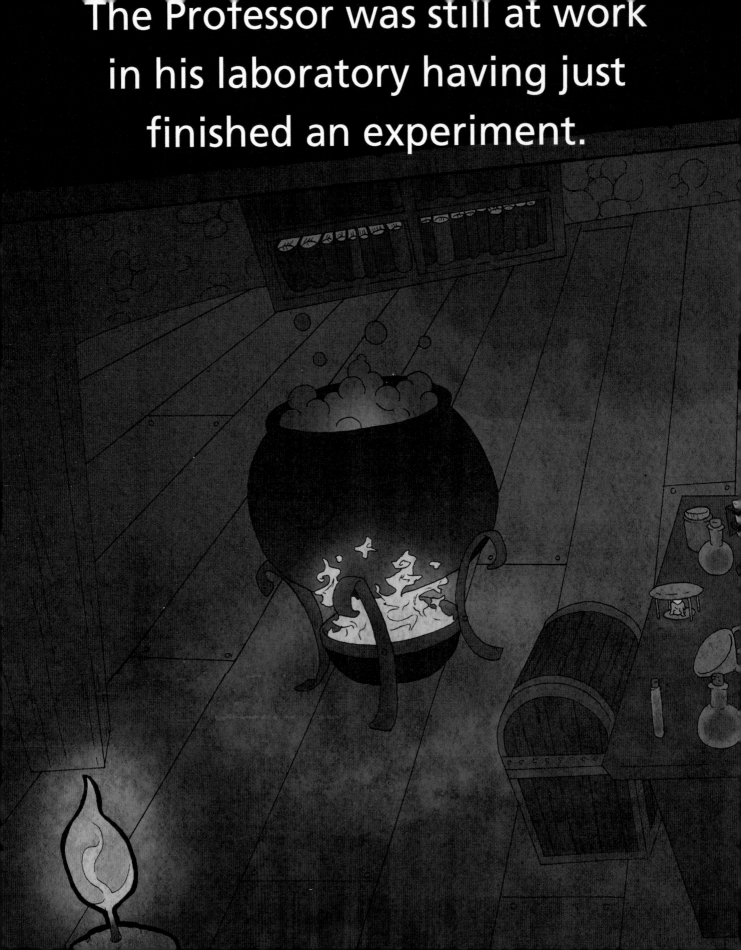

The Professor was still at work in his laboratory having just finished an experiment.

He believed that he had finally prepared a potion that when tasted would cause anyone or "anything" to grow in size.

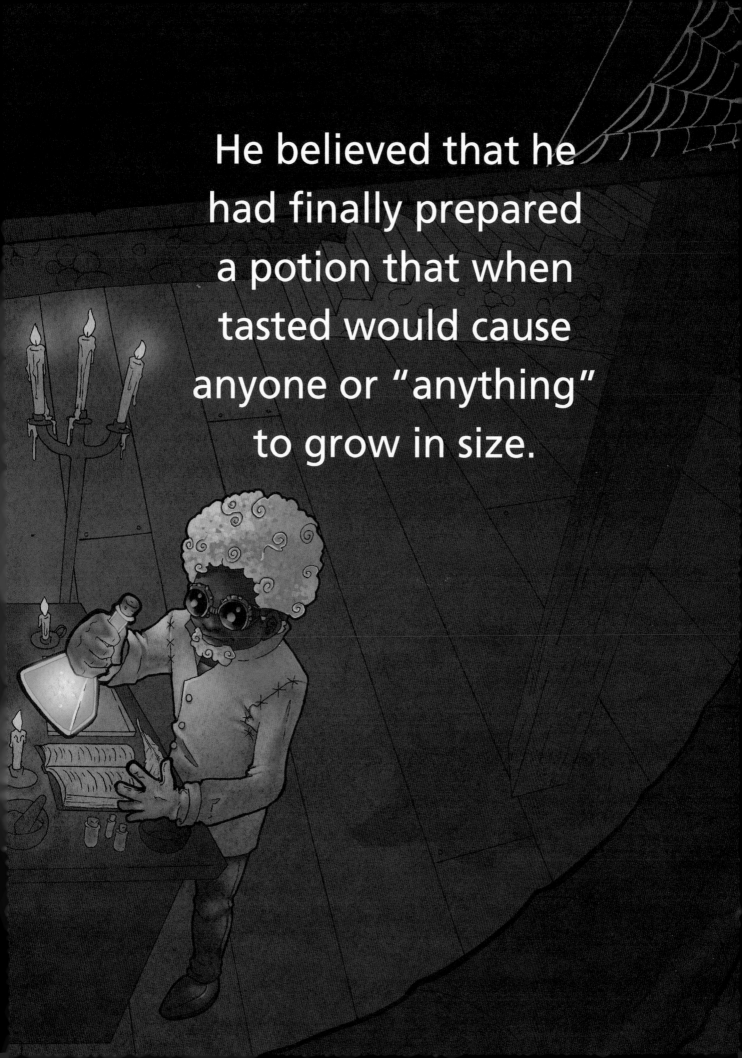

In his excitement, the professor dashed up the stairs and ran to his pet spider, Mark.

Mark was in a cage on the tabletop. Speaking as though the spider had human qualities, the Professor said,

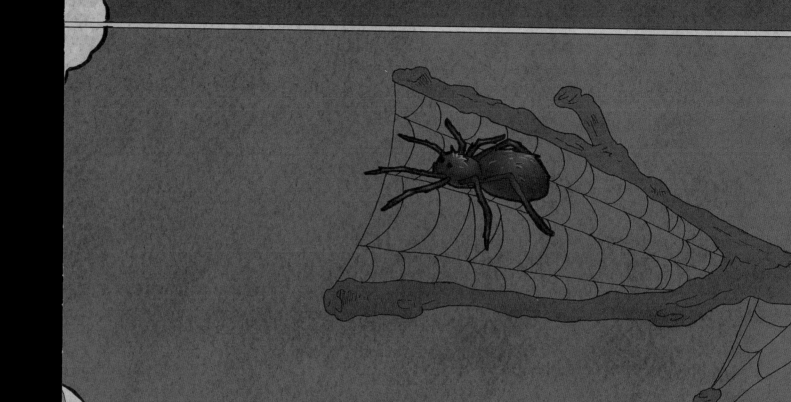

"If this works, people all over the world will buy my potion, and I will be rich, filthy rich, I say"!

The professor took Mark out of
the cage, placed him gently on
the table and let Mark
drink of this potion.

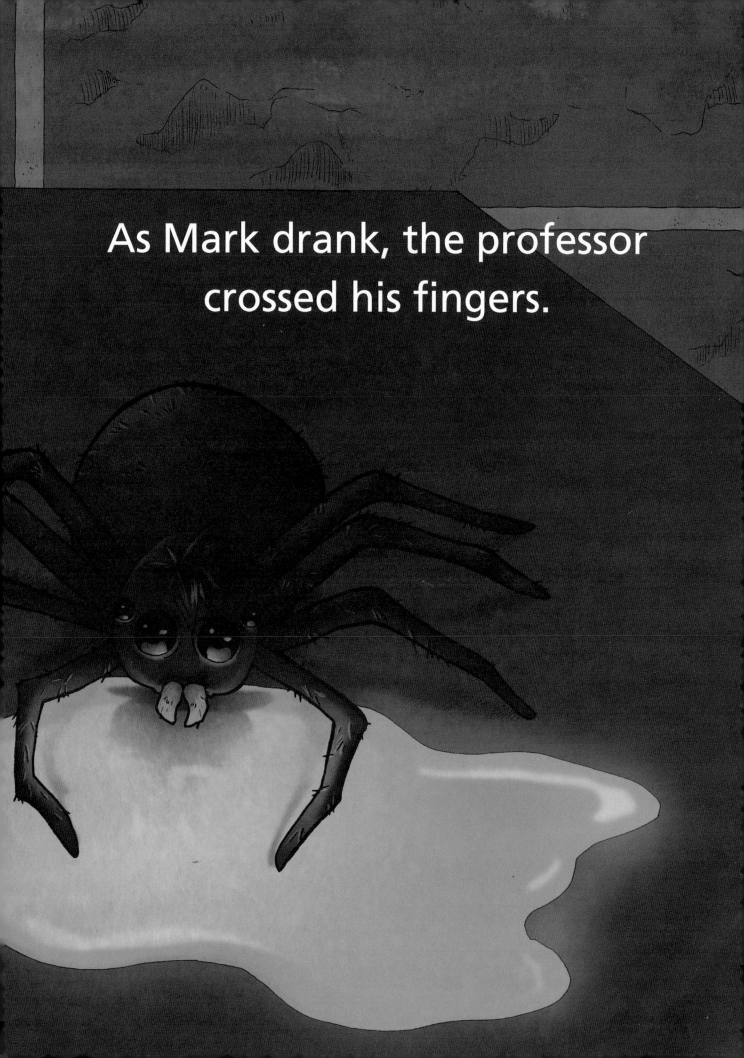

As Mark drank, the professor crossed his fingers.

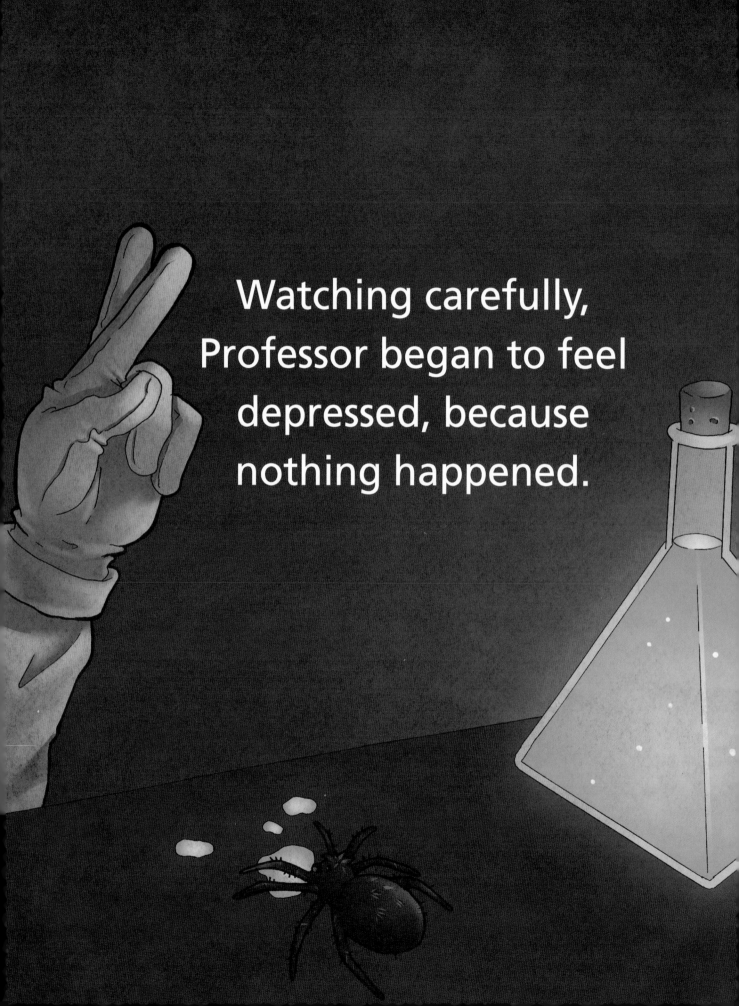

Watching carefully, Professor began to feel depressed, because nothing happened.

Putting all thoughts of becoming rich aside, the professor left Mark, and went to his bedroom feeling as though he had failed again as sleep overtook him.

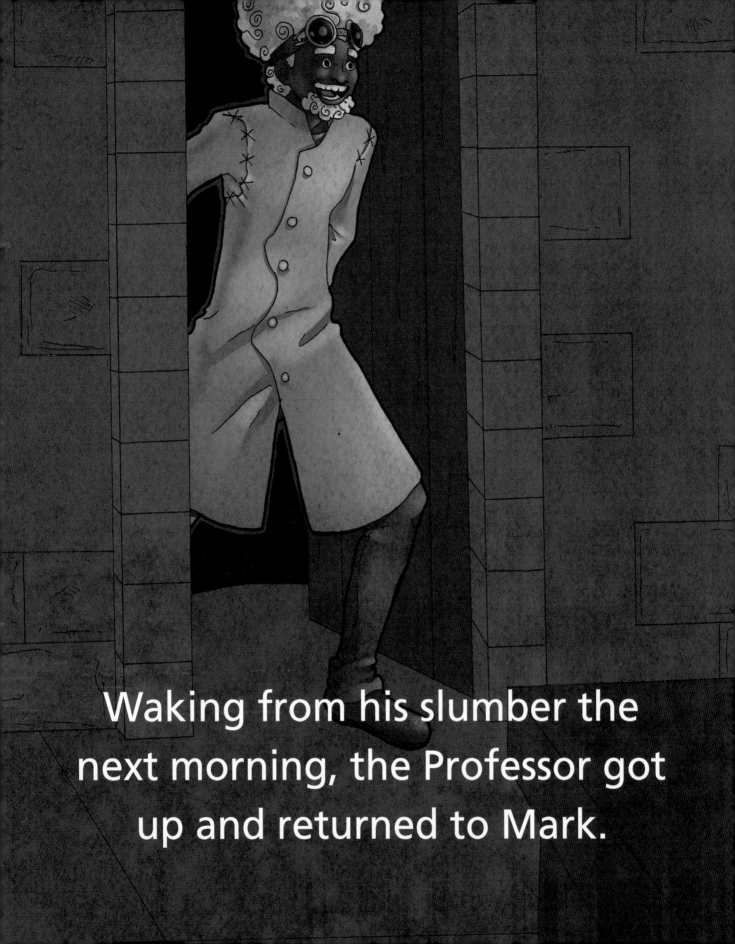

Waking from his slumber the next morning, the Professor got up and returned to Mark.

When he opened the door,
Professor saw his spider,
Mark had grown twice his size.

Amazed, Professor began to
shout all over the castle. No one
could have guessed his joy. "I've
done it, I'm going to be rich,
Mark", the professor said.

Mark gave a knowing smile and said, "I'm hungry"!

Professor was astonished for he did not know that Mark would also be able to speak.

Right away, the professor rushed to the kitchen and made some pancakes for himself and his new companion.

The professor gave Mark a nice cold glass of water.

"Oh, what have I done?
I have to figure out another
potion to return Mark
back to his normal size."

Mark became even hungrier and lost control. Mark broke down one of the castle walls looking for food as he headed for the small village.

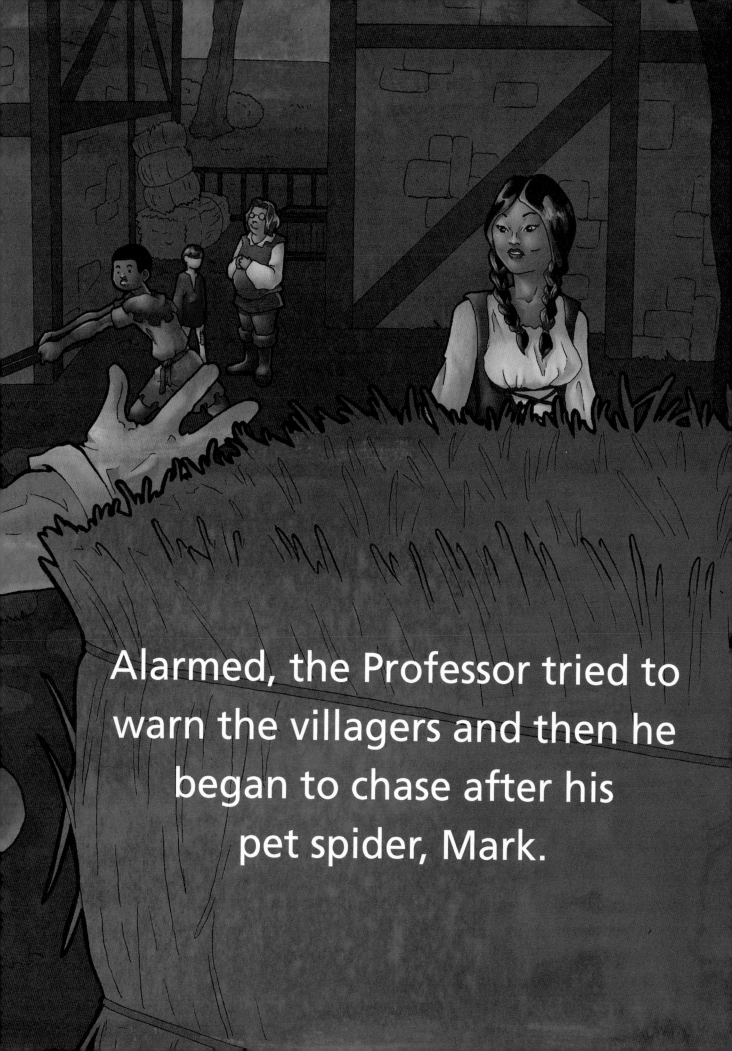

Alarmed, the Professor tried to warn the villagers and then he began to chase after his pet spider, Mark.

For a moment, Mark did not know what to do or which way to go. While he was thinking, the Professor grabbed onto one of his legs saying, "Stop", "Stop".

Mark stormed the village,
crushing the local bakery shop,

and then finding a food market,
he began to eat and eat.

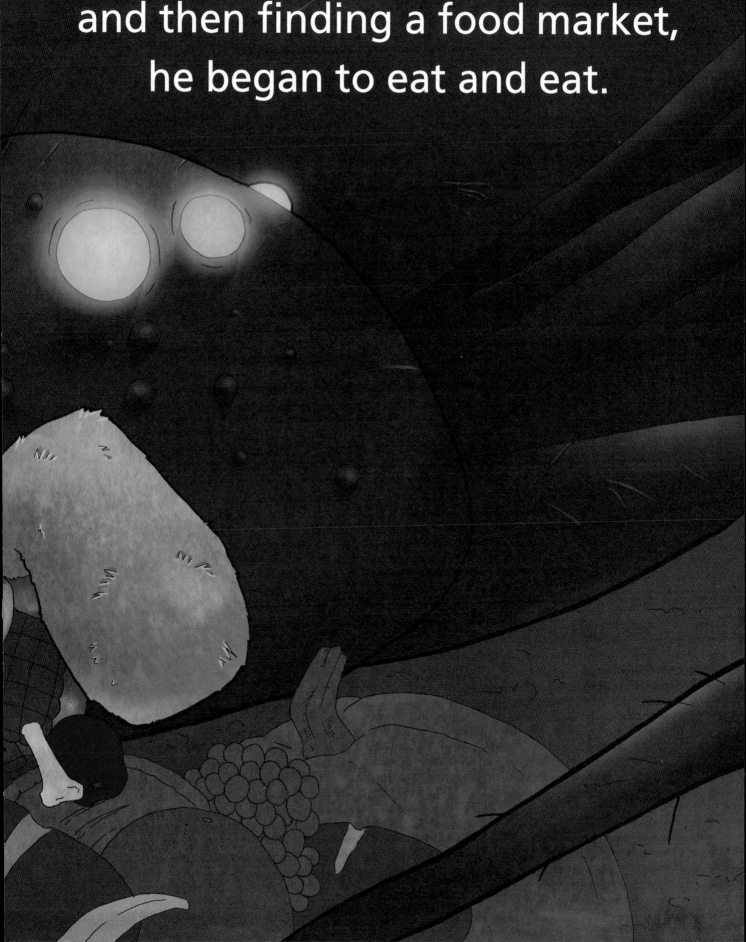

Mark lifted trucks that were delivering food and ate.

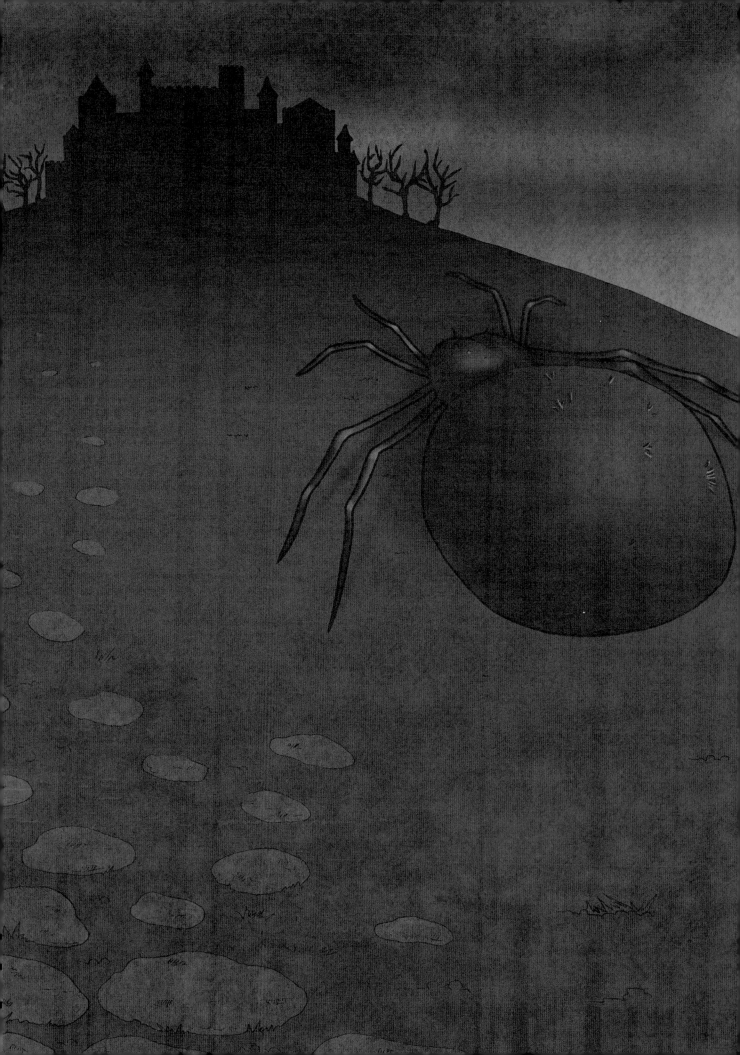

Satisfied, Mark turned away from the village and headed back to the only place he knew to be home, the professor's old castle.

Oddly enough, Mark went straight to the laboratory as if wanting this madness to stop.

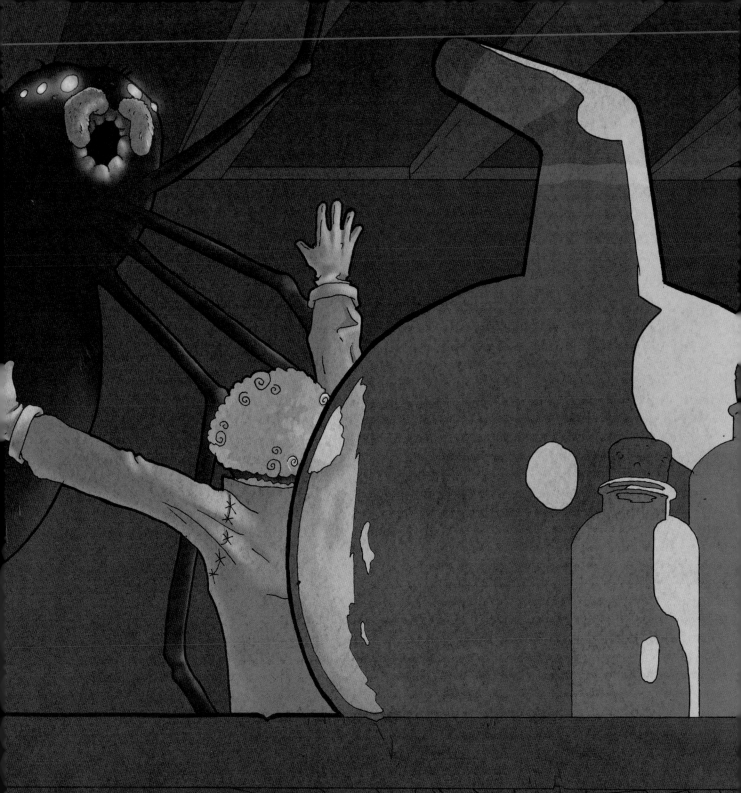

Professor followed closely behind
and tried to calm Mark down.

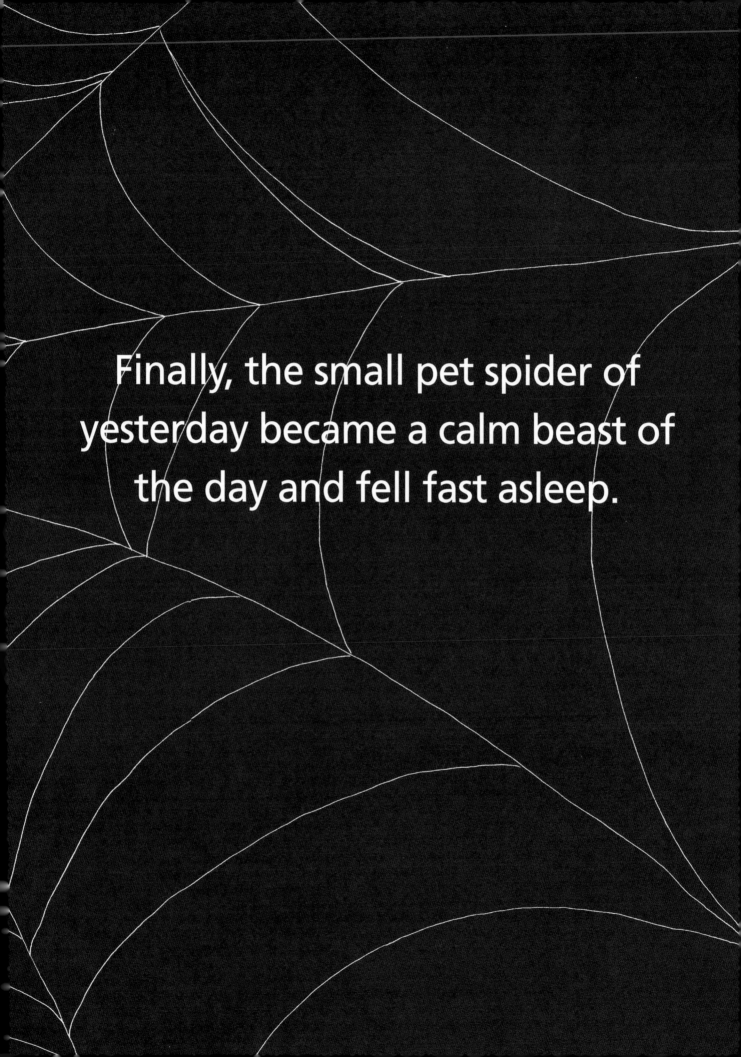

Finally, the small pet spider of yesterday became a calm beast of the day and fell fast asleep.

Soon the Professor could hear angry sounds from outside of the castle. The villagers came to the door saying, "let's get rid of this beast", and they began to chant, "let us kill the beast".

They chanted this
over and over again.

The Professor convinced the angry people to let him work on the problem for a few days.

Working day and night, the professor struggled to find a solution, and having found no solution, he prepared for bed.

As he was taking his pajamas
out of the drawer,
an idea struck him.

He sounded the village alarm to tell the whole village.

Everyone listened very close to what the professor was saying.

You see, the villagers were not able to grow and harvest the crops they needed to exist.

Therefore, Professor reminded the villagers of their problem. Mr. Gorman, the Baker, asked him how Mark would fit in helping them.

The professor quickly explained that with Mark's size and his extra legs, he could help plant, and help to reap during harvest to make sure everyone would have plenty of vegetables stored up for the winter.

Two, there would be much left for Mark's hunger attacks. Everyone thought this was a great idea, and Mark became a "hero" instead of the beast they all thought he was.

Mark worked hard and fast to plant crops and worked even harder during the time of harvest.

Everyone began to love Mark
and decided not to tell anyone
outside of their little village
about their good fortune.

There was enough food stored
for the people and for Mark.

All lived happily ever after.

The End

Made in the USA
Charleston, SC
15 March 2016